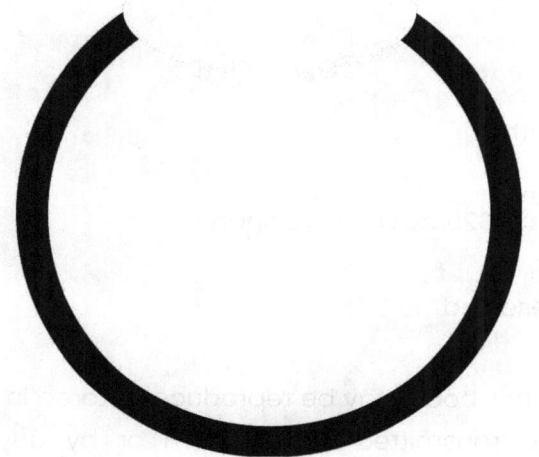

BEYOND TRUTH

Oliver Reinhart

Copyright

Beyond Truth

Copyright © 2025 by Oliver Reinhart
First Edition
All rights reserved.

No part of this book may be reproduced, stored in a retrieval system, or transmitted in any form or by any means—electronic, mechanical, photocopying, recording, or otherwise—without the prior written permission of the author, except in the case of brief quotations embodied in critical reviews and certain other noncommercial uses permitted by copyright law.

This is a work of nonfiction. While every effort has been made to ensure the accuracy of the information contained herein, the author makes no representations or warranties regarding the completeness or reliability of the content. The views and opinions expressed are those of the author and are intended for informational and educational purposes only. The reader is encouraged to seek professional advice where appropriate.

ISBN: 979-8-9920665-4-8

Author's Note
By Oliver Reinhart

This wasn't something I wrote.
It was something I uncovered — like stone beneath sand.

Not a political book. Not a call to arms.
Just a return to what you already know.

Piece by piece, it emerged — not as a manifesto, but as a mirror.
I've spent most of my life building, leading, questioning, and quietly watching the systems we all live within.
Some I helped grow. Some I walked away from. All of them taught me what this book now says:

Truth doesn't need to be proven.
It needs to be remembered.
And lived.

The first line came to me one night in silence —
a moment so still, it felt like the world exhaled.
That's when I knew this wasn't about teaching.
It was about translating something many of us already feel.

You've likely felt it too.
The distortion.
The loneliness that isn't really loneliness.
The quiet resonance of something real beneath all the noise.

This book is here to say:
You are not alone.
You were never the minority.
And you are not imagining what you see.

If it helps you trust that — in yourself, and in others —
then we're already walking in the world beyond this.
Thank you for meeting me here.

The signal is yours now.
The light is already being passed.

— Oliver Reinhart

Before You Begin

This is not a book of answers.
It is a mirror.
A quiet return.

If it feels strange at first, keep going.
The words are not here to explain —
but to reflect.

You do not need to agree.
You do not need to understand all at once.
You only need to feel what stays with you.

And if something echoes...

You were never the only one.

ACT I
The Illusion of Certainty

"What if everything you've been taught to trust was only part of the truth?"

Chapter: 01

The Circle

> Truth became institutionalized. Then it became controlled.

At first, the Circle seemed harmless.
Helpful, even.
It filtered information. Provided clarity. Protected us from chaos.

But something changed.

What began as a tool for understanding became a wall around truth.
What began as a lens became a cage.
Only what could be proven inside the Circle was allowed to exist.
Everything else?
Dismissed. Ignored. Mocked.

You've felt it.

That moment when your knowing wasn't accepted — because it wasn't cited.
That experience you couldn't explain — so it didn't count.
That intuition, that dream, that sudden understanding that got dismissed with:
"There's no proof."

Inside the Circle, truth isn't something you feel.
It's something you're granted — after permission, after data, after validation.

The Circle is policed by a belief:

> If it hasn't been proven by the system, it isn't real.

This belief didn't start with bad intentions.
But over time, it created a culture where perception was outsourced, curiosity was shamed, and experience was silenced.

You started doubting your own eyes.
You second-guessed your feelings.
You looked to institutions — science, media, academia, experts — not to inform your view…
but to approve it.

And anything outside that approved worldview?
Became dangerous.
Conspiratorial.
Naive.
Even when it rang true.

You stopped trusting what you knew.

You started living by what was allowed.
Like learning to trust ratings over your own hotel experience.
Or headlines over the way someone made you feel.
And slowly…
you stopped seeing what didn't fit inside the Circle.

Chapter: 02
The Proof Trap
When "proof" becomes permission.

At some point, proof stopped being about discovery.
And started being about **control**.

Proof used to be a process —
a way to test, to explore, to bring form to the formless.

But inside the Circle, it became a gate.
If your experience didn't pass through that gate —
it wasn't real.

You were told:
"Extraordinary claims require extraordinary evidence."

But what if the extraordinary can't be measured yet?
What if the evidence comes **after** the truth is felt?

What if you are the evidence?

Here's the trap:
The same system that defines what counts as "real"...
is also the one that gets to decide when it's proven.

Which means:
You can feel something with every cell in your body…
And still be told it's invalid.

Because it doesn't fit the structure.
Because it hasn't been studied.
Because it isn't on the approved list.

Proof became a weapon.
A silencer.
A way to hold power over experience — instead of honor it.

But here's what they never told you:
Most of the things we now call "proven"?
They started as someone's unprovable knowing.
The link between smoking and cancer? Laughed at for decades. The gut-brain connection? Woo-woo until it wasn't.

Someone trusted what they felt.
Long before it was accepted.
Long before it was safe.

And they kept going.

That's the real proof.

Chapter: 03

The Empire of Experts

The more we trusted them, the less we trusted ourselves.

Experts were meant to guide us.

They were supposed to help us see clearly,
to teach us what we couldn't yet explain.

And in many ways, they did.
They do.

But something shifted.

Somewhere along the way, experts became gatekeepers of reality.
And we — the people living that reality — were told to defer.

> *"You're not qualified."*
> *"You don't have the credentials."*
> *"Trust the science."*
> *Even when it changed. Eggs were bad, then good. Coffee dangerous, then protective.*

Even when the experts disagreed.
Even when your own body, your own eyes, your own heart told you something different.

We stopped asking,
"Does this feel true?"
And started asking,
"Is this what I'm supposed to believe?"

That's when the Empire was built.

An empire of PhDs and podiums.
Of headlines and algorithms.
Of formulas that proved something we hadn't actually lived.

And if you questioned it?
You weren't thinking.
You were dangerous.

This isn't about discrediting intelligence.
Or expertise.
Or science.

It's about remembering:

Wisdom isn't the same as authority.
Experience isn't less valid than education.

Truth doesn't belong to experts.
It belongs to everyone willing to look — really look — at what is.

Even if it hasn't been explained yet.
Even if no one else sees it.
Yet.

Chapter: 04
The Lie of Being Alone

You weren't the only one. You were just the only one who didn't stay quiet.

How many times have you felt it —
a moment of clarity so sharp it startled you?

You saw through something.
Felt something.
Knew something you weren't supposed to know.

And then you told someone.
Or tried to.
And they blinked. Smiled politely. Changed the subject.

So you said nothing the next time.
And the next.

And slowly, you began to believe the oldest lie in the Circle:
> *"I'm the only one who sees this."*

But here's the truth:

You are not the only one.

You never were.

Millions of people have felt what you felt.
They've noticed the same cracks.
Heard the same dissonance.
Seen the same distortion between what's said... and what's real.

That feeling right before an earthquake. Or sensing someone was gone before the phone rang.

But they didn't speak.

Not because they didn't know.
But because they didn't feel safe.

So they nodded.
Laughed at the joke.
Played the part.
Kept the knowing quiet.

Silence isn't the absence of truth.
It's often a symptom of fear.

We were trained to believe that truth must be validated before it's spoken.
And so we swallowed it.
Held it.
Pretended not to know what we knew.

And that's how the Circle stayed strong:
Not because we were wrong.
But because we believed we were alone.
You weren't.

**ACT II
The Awakening**

"What if truth was always within you
- just waiting to be trusted?"

Chapter: 05

The Many Ways of Knowing

Truth doesn't have one voice. It has a symphony.

You were taught that the only way to know something was to prove it — with logic, evidence, and consensus.

But that's not how you've really lived.

You've known things with your gut.
You've known things through grief.
You've known things before they happened.
You've known things you couldn't explain — but couldn't deny.

And you were right.

There are **many ways of knowing.**

Some people know through logic — clean, structured, deductive.
Others know through emotion — the full-body yes or the deep internal no.

Some know through lived experience — the body doesn't lie.
Others know through intuition — that silent, instantaneous recognition.
Some feel it in art.
Some feel it in silence.
Some feel it in movement, in sound, in the space between people.

None of these ways are superior.
None of them are lesser.
They are different **frequencies** of truth.

And the moment you stop ranking them —
you begin to see the whole picture.

The Circle told you that only certain kinds of knowing were " real."
But you've always known more than that.

You just didn't have permission.

Until now.

Like hearing a song you've never heard and crying anyway.

Chapter: 06

The Mirror

Truth doesn't always teach. It reflects.

You've spent your life looking for someone to explain it to you.
To tell you what's true.
To give you the words that finally make sense.

But what if the most powerful truths…
don't arrive as answers?

What if they arrive as **recognition**?

You read something — and your body says yes.
You hear a story — and something in you softens.
You see a stranger — and feel like you've met before.

These moments don't teach.
They reflect.
They *mirror* something that was already there — but waiting to be seen.

That's what awakening is.

Not discovering something new.
But remembering something old.

Something buried under fear, approval, and noise.

You don't have to argue with the Circle anymore.
You don't have to win.

You just have to **look directly at what you already know** —
and stop pretending you don't see it.

The way your stomach turned before the deal went wrong.
The peace you felt when you said yes — even when no one else did.

That's where truth begins.
Not with evidence.
But with resonance.
You won't always be able to explain it.
But you'll feel it.

And that is enough.

Chapter: 07

The New Compass

When truth becomes internal, so does direction.

After you remember, everything shifts.
Not in the world — not yet.
But inside.

You stop searching for approval.
You stop waiting for proof.
You stop asking others which way to go.

Because something new begins to guide you:
Resonance.

It's subtle.
It's quiet.
But it's unmistakable.

You know when something feels aligned.
You know when something feels distorted.

Not because someone told you.
But because your whole being recognizes the frequency.

This is your new compass.

It's not mapped.
It's not standardized.
It's not always easy to explain.

But it's yours.
And it never lies.

You'll still hear the noise of the Circle.
You'll still feel the pull of doubt.

But over time, the signal gets stronger.
The noise gets quieter.
And you learn to navigate not by what's allowed…
but by what's *true*.
Even if no one else understands.
Even if you don't have the words.

Like the moment you knew you had to walk away — from the job, the partner, the story.

You are not lost.
You are remembering how to move.

Chapter: 08

The Upgrade

> You're not broken. You're just tuning to a new frequency.

The Circle taught you that change means rebellion.
That stepping outside the system means you're confused, unstable, lost.

But awakening isn't rebellion.
It's **evolution**.

You're not glitching.
You're upgrading.

Your body is clearer.
Your relationships shift.
You don't tolerate distortion the way you used to.

You say less — but mean more.
You stop trying to convince.
You start listening more deeply.

And even though your outer life may look the same...
your inner posture has changed.

You're no longer seeking truth.
You're living from it.

This is not the end of your journey.
It's the beginning of a new one.

A life without performance.
Without pretending.
Without waiting for permission to feel what you feel.

And as more people awaken,
you begin to notice something...

You're not alone.

ACT III
The Return of Truth

"You were never the minority. You were just the first one willing to speak."

Chapter: 09

The Silent Majority

> You're not the only one who knows. You're just the only one who said it out loud.

You've felt alone for a long time.

Not because your truth is rare —
but because few people say theirs out loud.

This is how the system survived:
Not by convincing everyone...
but by keeping everyone convinced they were alone.
But you weren't.

You were just one of the first to speak.

Behind every quiet doubt is a person holding back.
Behind every held breath is a knowing that never found its voice.
Behind every dinner table silence...
is a memory, a pattern, a truth *someone else saw too* — but swallowed.

You've met them.

They're the ones who pause too long before answering.
Like the friend who almost says 'I don't believe this either,' but swallows it at the last second.
The ones who almost say something — then don't.
The ones who glance across the room when the topic gets close.

They saw it too.
They felt it too.

But they were waiting.

Waiting for someone else to speak first.
Waiting for someone else to make it okay.
Waiting to know they weren't crazy.

You were never the minority.
You were just the **first one willing to speak.**

The Circle never needed to erase truth.
It only needed to isolate it.
To scatter the knowers.
To make sure no two stood close enough to **recognize each other.**

But that's changing now.

You're beginning to see them.
In the eyes of strangers.
In the hesitation before a sentence.
In the softness after a moment of courage.

You're not the exception.
You're not the voice in the wilderness.

You're part of something.
Quiet.
Massive.
Already in motion.

And when someone finally says it —
just says it —
not to preach, not to persuade,
but simply to be honest...

Something shifts.

Not a rebellion.
Not a performance.
Just a quiet ripple.

A glance. A breath. A signal passed not in language...
but in recognition.

A symbol not yet spoken.
A light not yet named.
But seen.

And once it's seen — it cannot be unseen.

> *You were never the minority.*
> *You were just the first one willing to speak.*

Chapter: 10

The Language of Light

How symbols, stories, and silence awaken more than arguments ever could.

The Circle taught us to explain everything.
To win debates.
To cite.
To prove.

But truth doesn't spread by force.
It spreads by **resonance**.

And resonance doesn't need evidence.
It needs presence.

You've felt it:
- A glance that said everything.
  Like that look exchanged across a room when someone says *something we both know isn't true.*
- A story that felt like a memory.
- A hand over the heart that softened the whole room.

No pitch.
No proof.
Just presence.

That's the new language.

Light doesn't shout.
It doesn't persuade.

It reveals.
It warms.
It *reminds*.

When you stand in truth, you transmit it.
Even in silence.
Especially in silence.

And when someone else is ready...
They feel it.
Even if they don't understand it yet.

That's how truth travels now.
Not by doctrine.
But by **recognition**.

You don't have to teach.
You don't have to argue.

You just have to **live in alignment.**
And let your signal shine —
unapologetic, unproven, uncontained.

Because the more light we share,
the more clearly we all begin to see.

You weren't meant to walk in the dark.

You were meant to be the light others remember by.

Chapter: 11

The Circle Dissolves

> What no longer controls you, no longer defines you.

You don't have to fight the Circle.
You just have to **stop feeding it.**

It doesn't survive on truth.
It survives on attention.
On your hesitation.
On your fear of being wrong.

But the moment you see it clearly...
you stop playing the game.

And that's when it begins to dissolve.

The Circle isn't defeated by protest.
It fades through disuse.
Like a bridge no one walks anymore.
Like a throne no one kneels to.

You stop asking for permission.
You stop seeking validation.
You stop checking if the system approves of your steps.

And suddenly...
you're free.

Every time you choose alignment over approval —
the Circle loses power.

Every time you trust your knowing over consensus —
it weakens.

Every time you speak without waiting to be invited —
it crumbles.

Not because you fought it.
But because you stopped needing it.

It can still shout.
It can still spin.
It can still demand attention.

But without your agreement —
it's just noise.

What once controlled you...
now just spins in the background.

Loud, maybe.
But irrelevant.

> *You didn't fight the Circle.*
> *You just stopped needing its permission to exist.*

Chapter: 12
The World After This

What it looks like when truth is no longer owned.

The Circle is gone.

Not because it was defeated.
But because it became irrelevant.

What once ruled everything...
now just sits quietly in the background.

You walk past it without anger.
Without fear.
Without needing to explain why.

It simply...
doesn't apply to you anymore.

This isn't a perfect world.
But it's a **clearer** one.

People still disagree.
They still get lost.
They still forget.

But something is different.

There are fewer masks.
More pauses.
More people saying what they mean — instead of what they're supposed to say.

Fewer performances.

More presence.
There's less content. More contact.

You stop asking who's in charge.
Because you don't need someone else to hold the key anymore.

You're not waiting.
You're not convincing.
You're just... living.

In alignment.
In clarity.
In truth.

This isn't a revolution.
It's a **return.**

A quiet return
to dignity,
to direct experience,
to self-trust.

Some people stay in the Circle.
That's okay.

The new world doesn't argue.
It *exists*.

And when someone is ready,
they'll see it.

You don't have to bring them.

You just have to be visible when they arrive.

> *The Circle is gone.*
> *The signal is clear.*
> *And the world —*
> *is already remembering.*

APPENDIX

Living Beyond Truth: A Guide for the Awake

A practical compass for those who remember.

You don't need more advice.
You need space to practice what you already know.
This guide isn't for awakening.
It's for **living from the place you've already reached** —
without falling back into the Circle.
No rules. No dogma.
Just orientation.

1. Recognizing the Circle in Real Life

The Circle often looks like:

- Needing consensus before you act
- Feeling shame when your experience doesn't match what's accepted
- Explaining your truth to make it valid
- Asking for permission before moving

It's not just a system.
It's a reflex.
Just noticing it... begins to release it.

2. Disengaging Without Conflict

You don't need to argue.
You don't need to convince.
You don't need to "wake people up."
You can simply stop participating.

- Change the subject
- Choose a different room
- Say nothing at all

Hold your knowing —
without offering it for validation.

3. Making Decisions from Resonance

Don't ask: *What should I do?*
Ask: *What feels aligned in my body?*
If it feels heavy, distorted, defensive — pause.
If it feels clear, calm, light — move.
Your body knows.
Your silence knows.
Resonance never shouts.

4. When Others Challenge Your Truth

They will.
You don't have to defend it.
Just say:
"That's not how it feels to me."
Then move on.
You're not here to win.
You're here to stay aligned.

5. Raising Children Without Rebuilding the Circle
Teach them:
- Their emotions are valid
- Their experience matters
- Silence can be sacred
- Truth doesn't need approval

Let them become mirrors — not followers.

6. Leading, Loving, and Living Without Control
Let go of:
- Needing to be understood
- Fear of being wrong
- Trying to be above or below anyone

Lead by living clearly.
Love by staying present.
Live by trusting what you feel.

7. Daily Practices to Stay Awake
- Begin your day with silence
- Ask: Am I speaking from truth or fear?
- End your day with: What did I know today that I didn't say? Why not?

Freedom is a habit.

8. Recognizing Others in the Silent Majority
You'll know them by:
- The pause before they speak
- The softness in their eyes
- The quiet yes in their presence

You don't need a handshake.
Just a moment of honesty.
Say something real.
You might unlock them.

9. Final Invocation

You don't need to speak louder.
You don't need to be right.
You don't need to change the world.
You just need to **live in alignment** with what you now know.
The rest will follow.
You are not alone.
You were never the minority.
And you're already walking in the world beyond this.

The Gesture

If you ever wish to signal this truth — not through words, but through presence — form **a broken circle** with your hands:

- Your thumbs and index fingers meet to shape a circle...
- ...but the index fingertips don't touch.
- Leave a small gap at the top — a breath of light between them.

This is not a brand.
It's not a secret.
It's a reminder:

> *"I see. I remember. I'm awake."*

No one will tell you when to use it.
You'll know.

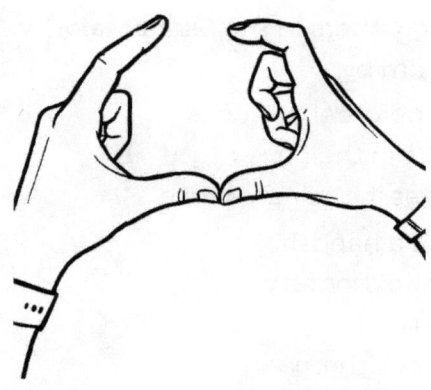

www.ingramcontent.com/pod-product-compliance
Lightning Source LLC
Chambersburg PA
CBHW070047070426
42449CB00012BA/3177